YES, ALEXANDER?

POEMS

Thomas Peter Bennett

Goose River Press
Waldoboro, Maine

Copyright © 2024 Thomas Peter Bennett

All rights reserved. No part of this book may be reproduced in any form without written permission from the publisher, except by a reviewer who may quote brief passages in a review to be printed in a newspaper or magazine.

ISBN: 978-1-59713-278-7 Paperback
ISBN: 978-1-59713-279-4 Hardcover

First Printing, 2024

Published by
Goose River Press
3400 Friendship Road
Waldoboro ME 04572
e-mail: gooseriverpress@gmail.com
www.gooseriverpress.com

AUTHOR'S NOTES

Alexander, Alex or Al, depending on time and circumstance, was the source of these life poems.

I thank him for his words, thoughts, and permission to publish them in this collection of dialog poems, of my response, "Yes, Alexander?" to his thoughtful questions or comments over time. And to his mother, my wife over these many wonderful years.

Thanks also to Deborah Benner for her editorial guidance and publishing several of these poems in *Goose River Anthologies*.

Thomas Peter Bennett
Silver Spring, Maryland, 2024

CONTENTS

AMELIORATION OF HIS VOCABULARY 1

BABY PIGEON OR A SPARROW? 2

PERPLEXED BY A FEDERAL GRANT REPORT IN
                         OUR CAR'S BACKSEAT 3

IT AIN'T LIKE TALLAHASSEE 4

READY FOR SCHOOL 6

AN ABANDONED CASTLE 7

ARCO ON THE SCHUYLKILL 8

NOT A PLUMBER 9

GONE TO CAMP 10

AN OUTING 11

MONEY FOR MOVIES 13

TO THE FORGE 14

PERPLEXING CONVERSATION 15

HOW? WHY? 16

IN GEORGIA 17

LOVE TEARS 19

ALEX'S QUERY 20

WRITING WORKSHOP CONVERSATION 21

CONTENTS

SEEKING A SOLUTION 22

DRIVING UP TO PHILLY 23

AGE DIFFERENCE 24

AN ORCHID FOR MOM 25

FLOWERS FOR MOM 26

MOTHER'S DAY CODA 27

YES, ALEXANDER?

AMELIORATION OF HIS VOCABULARY
–Alexander, age 4–

Daddy!
  Do you know what
  Men witches are called?   *He queried,*
                              While wearing his ski mask.

What,
  Alexander?   I quizzed.

Woodcocks!   *He shouted.*

No,
  Alexander;
  Warlocks!   I coached.

Ho! Ho!   *He chortled.*

BABY PIGEON OR A SPARROW?
–Alexander, age 4–

Look, Daddy.
  A baby pigeon!   *He cried out*
                                During our park walk.

I'm not sure, Alexander,
  It may be a sparrow.   I suggested.

  Or is it a baby pigeon?   I thought,
                                  Although, they are
                                  Seldom seen.

PERPLEXED BY A FEDERAL GRANT REPORT IN OUR CAR'S BACKSEAT
–Alexander, age 5–

                                        Night drive to the university,
                                        Talking in the dark

Daddy,
  How many big dictionaries
  Do we have?   *He questioned.*
                                          From the back seat.

Two, Alexander!
  One in my office
  And one at home.   *I recalled.*

Daddy,
  How many big Bibles
  Do we have?   *He continued.*

Two, Alexander!
  Our family Bible and
  One that Granny gave us.   *I confirmed.*

Then, Daddy,
  What's this big book back here?

IT AIN'T LIKE TALLAHASSEE
–Alexander, age 5–

                    As we walked along the Parkway,
                    He declared,

Daddy,
   It's different in Philadelphia.

Yes, Alexander.
                    I granted, as
                    I pulled my scarf snugly
                    Around my neck.

The buildings are bigger,
   Museums are everywhere.
                    He remarked,
                    Quietly singing
                    Zip-a-Dee-Doodah.

It's colder,
   Buildings are more decorated.
                    He mock shivered,
                    Hopping from one sidewalk plate
                    To the next.

I know, Alexander.
                    I agreed,
                    Pulling my scarf tighter.

There are more statues,
   Not as many trees.
                    He opined,
                    Quietly continuing to sing
                    Zip-a-Dee-Doodah.

It's colder,
   Cars are everywhere.   He noted
                    As he hopped and sang.

Car tags are different.
   There's a piece of ice.   *He pointed.*

It ain't like Tallahassee!
It ain't like Tallahassee! We chorused.

READY FOR SCHOOL
-Alexander, age 5-

                        Looking in the mirror,
                        He declared,

Daddy!
  I've got two shirts
      On.

Yes. Alexander?   I observed.

Daddy!
  I've got two front
      Teeth.
                        His mirrored glance
                        Confirmed.

Yes, Alexander.   I concurred.

I'm ready for
    School!   He crowed.

AN ABANDONED CASTLE
–Alexander, age 8–

Daddy!	*He exclaimed* *During our night walk.*
Yes, Alexander?	I acknowledged, Glancing at the Academy.
Your buildings *Look like real buildings!*	*He shouted,* *Looking at its sparkling bricks.*
Yes, Alexander!	I confirmed, Gazing at the Academy.
When we moved to Philadelphia,	*He recalled,* *Peering toward Logan Circle,*
The Academy looked like *An abandoned castle!*	*He declared.*
Yes, Alexander.	I remembered… Staring at the new façade, Thinking of the work Yet to be done,

ARCO ON THE SCHUYLKILL
–Alex, age 10–

Dad!
  What are those big tanks?   Alex quizzed.

They're filled with
  Gas and oil.   I responded,
                                   Glancing at the tanks.

Then why is there a
  Gas shortage?   He questioned,
                                   Staring at the fields of
                                   Storage tanks.

The needs are very great!   I explained, outlining
                                   Supply and demand.

But Dad,
  Have they measured
  The contents of each tank?

NOT A PLUMBER
–Alex, age 10–

Water spewing everywhere!	Alex watches.
I try to tighten this bolt.	Damn it!
Try to counter that leak.	Damn it!

Plumbing has many interlinked,
                Interconnected,
                Female and
                Male
                Connections

All are leaking.	Damn it!
As I seek a Rosetta stone For stoppage.	Damn it!

Dad, be glad you're
  Not a plumber.
                                        Alex comments
                                        As he watches.

GONE TO CAMP
–Alex, age 10–

It's quiet at home.

Dinner is peaceful.

The TV is off.

The turtle, dog, fish, snake,
   And plants

It's too quiet at home.

Alex has gone to camp.

No shouts.

No criticism.

No gripes.

Want Alex's attention
And care.

Shouts and beefs
Are missed.

AN OUTING
–Alex, age 11–

Morning

Dad!	He shouted, Standing at our bedroom door At 7:30 Sunday morning.
Yes, Alex?	Startled awake, I Glanced at the clock.
It's a beautiful day!	He yelled, Opening the curtains, Flooding in light.
We're going to the beach! Yes?	He announced, Raising the possibility.
Wake me at 8:30!	Pulling the curtain cord, And grabbing my pillow.
I'll talk to Mom,	Who lay sleeping.
Dad! It's a beautiful day!	He shouted at 8:30, While wearing a swimsuit.

Afternoon

Dad! Are there sharks near us?	He called, Imploring, as Algae floated by.

No, Alex!

Dad!
  Is my chest tanning?

Yes, Alex.

I affirmed,
Confident and hopeful.

He anxiously questioned
As he lay on the beach,
Face covered with a towel.

I responded, glancing at
His pink splotches and
My 4:00 watch face.

MONEY FOR THE MOVIES
–Alex, age 12–

Dad,
  I need money!   *He announced.*

What for,
  Alex?   *I grilled.*

The movies!
  It's a dollar for a child
  And two dollars for an adult!   *He effused.*

So, Alex,
  Is it one or two?   *I probed.*

Even though,
  I'm a child,   *He declared,*

They may think,
  I'm an adult.   *He added.*

  Ok,
    Alex.   *I conceded.*

Here's two;
  Have fun!

TO THE FORGE
–Alex, age 12–

Dad,
  I can't wait!   *Alex exclaimed.*

Yes,
  Alex!   I understood.

I want to be
  A gold star student.   *He affirmed.*

Valley Forge is
  Going to be fun!   *He gushed.*

Yes,
  Alex!   I asserted.

I want to study
  Without distraction.   *He declared.*

I want to be a person of
  Good character.   *He pledged.*

I want to be a
  Leader.   *He added.*

You will,
  Alex!   I confirmed.

PERPLEXING CONVERSATION
–Alex, age 14–

As we drove home
From the Forge,

Dad, *Alex expounded.*
  You see,
    I've changed roommates;
    It's Portnof now.

After two years? I queried.

Yes,
  Portnof needs a gap filled. *He explained.*

Yes? I inquired.

Motivation is essential! *He declared.*

Yes,
  It is! I agreed,
  Perplexed.

Portnof needs motivation;
  He's my new assignment. *He proclaimed.*

HOW? WHY?
–Alex, age 18–

Alex on the telephone:

Dad,
You're home from Pittsburgh early.

                Yes, Alex, my back concerns me.
                The doc will check it out tomorrow.

                How is your cycling going?

Fine, Dad.

                And your money for the California races?

Don't worry, Dad.
It's coming together.

                Great, Alex,
                That's good news.

Putting my luggage down,

                I should have
                Asked,
                "How?"

Alex had sounded nervous.

                I should have
                Asked,
                "Why?"

IN GEORGIA
–Alex, age 19–

        At 10 pm,
        The telephone rang…

Dad. We broke down.	He announced.
Where are you?	I queried.
In a phone booth,	
404-789-3300,	
On Route 106,	
Fifteen miles from Athens.	He detailed.
Two longhairs	
In a VW van,	
Stuck on a Georgia road.	I reflected.
Be careful.	I warned.

        With a twenty-year memory trace
        Of a freedom ride in Georgia…

OK, Dad!
We don't like it here either.

We're trying to get	
The damn van started.	He added.
Are there other cars on the 106?	I probed.
Yes, Dad.	
Why the concern?	He questioned.

          A twenty-year flashback, unstated.

Be careful.   I said quickly.

Dad, don't worry,
We're trying to get
The van started.   *He replied at once.*

          A later telephone call and
          Further conversation...

Did you try a tow...?   I inquired,
I'll pay...   I suggested.

Thanks, Dad.
We can sleep in the van.
We'll get a tow tomorrow.   *He explained.*

Be careful!   I cautioned immediately.

Be careful!   I urged again.

We will be, Dad!

LOVE TEARS
–Alex, age 20–

Weeping,
Pleading,

For an escape
From fragmented love,
No more. No more. No more…

The end,
But not divorce.
A parting,

From love, not marriage.

Man tears,
Strong tears,
Often unrecognized,

Know love.

ALEX'S QUERY
–Alex, age 20–

Cliché
    or
        Verity,

Dad?

WRITING WORKSHOP CONVERSATION
-Al, age 21-

Dad,   *He warned.*

You'll be humiliated.
Don't risk it.
Workshops are the pits.

           Wisdom of a college junior in an English program.

Al,   I posed,
Humiliation is a daily thing,
It's part of life.

Life's a risk.

I've decided on a new venture.

SEEKING A SOLUTION...
–Al, age 22–

Hi, Mom.

Hi, Dad.

I've got a solution to

All my problems.

                        Yes...? and

                        What is it, Alex?

                        In unanimity on the phone.

I've got a puppy, and

His name is Floyd!

DRIVING UP TO PHILLY
–Al, age 22–

VW van, tuned up.

U-Haul trailer, linked up.
Books and computer, packed up.
Floyd in passenger seat, sitting up.
I-75 and -95 to Philly, driving up…
From Florida, all is up.

AGE DIFFERENCE
–Al, age 25–

If I had talked
To Alex,
Who is 25,

When I was 25,
Rather than now
When I am 55…

Our conversation would
Have a different tone.
At 25, I sounded like
Alex at 25.

Thirty years
Make a difference.

AN ORCHID FOR MOM
–Al, age 48–

A phone call from Alex—
    Hi, Dad, tomorrow's Mother's Day
    And I've been thinking about Mom,
    But I haven't had time to get a card
    Or send anything.
Every year, from
    Wherever he was at the time,
    Would you pick up an orchid
    For Mom…?
As the years passed,
    On every Saturday
Before Mother's Day,
    I always anticipated a call
And had an orchid in the garage…
But this Saturday,
    The orchid stands
Beside his card and the package
    That Amazon just delivered.
I'll miss his last minute phone call,
    And she will be surprised
On Mother's Day.

FLOWERS FOR MOM
–Al, age 53–

"The front desk just phoned, . .
    she exclaimed,
There are flowers for me at the desk!"

"Not from me!
    I explained.

Later,
    she returned with
a large vase of vase flowers
    and a birthday card
from Alex.

Yes, Alex,
    I reflected.

MOTHER'S DAY CODA
–Al, age 54–

"The front desk just phoned, . .
    she exclaimed,
There are flowers for me at the desk!"

No surprise. . . from me!
    I thought.

Later,
    she returned with
a large vase of tulips,
    chocolate candy
and a card.
"Happy Mother's Day. . .
    Alex, Honoria, and Lou!"
Yes, Alex.

ABOUT THE AUTHOR

Thomas Peter Bennett is a Florida native, former professor and natural history museum executive, he has published scientific articles and books, as well as poems and collections.

A graduate of Florida State University, Bennett earned his PhD in biochemistry from Rockefeller University and became an assistant professor at Harvard University. He later returned to FSU as a professor and the chair of biological sciences, afterwards serving as the special assistant to the president and acting executive vice president. His museum work began with his appointment as the president of the Academy of Natural Sciences of Philadelphia, now the Academy of Natural Sciences of Drexel University. After a decade at the Academy, he returned to Florida as a dean, professor, and the director of the Florida Museum of Natural History at the University of Florida. Ten years later he became the executive director of the South Florida Museum and retired as an emeritus executive director.

While teaching, Bennett started publishing poetry, attended workshops, and studied with Mary Oliver at Bennington College. Bennett's poems have appeared in, *Red Owl, Chebacco, POETALK, The Café Review, Puckerbrush Review, Pegasus Review,* and *Perspectives in Biology and Medicine*, among others, and in various anthologies, such as *Goose River Anthology, Cosmos Club Poets Through the Years,* and *Bay Area Poets Coalition*. He is the author of several poetry chapbooks and ten poetry books, including Nature, *As One Sees It (2003), A Celebration of John and William Bartram: In Philadelphia and Florida (2005), Hike On (2008), Encore Seasons (2017, Florida Sketches (2019), The Applause of Science (2021* and *Audubon Explores Florida (2023).*

In addition to his poetry and scientific works, Bennett has several textbooks and historical scientific books to his credit: *The Legacy: South Florida Museum (2010), Florida Explored: The Philadelphia Connection in Bartram's Tracks (2019)*. He is a member of The Explorers Club and the Cosmos Club.

His son, Dr. Alexander Staub Bennett is Research Professor and Director, Opioid Overdose Prevention Program at New York University, School of Global Public Health. Recipient 2018, New York City Department of Health, "Lifesaver Award." The author of many historical and scientific articles about drug addiction and harm reduction, he is a leader in establishing harm reduction centers.

www.ingramcontent.com/pod-product-compliance
Lightning Source LLC
Chambersburg PA
CBHW030534080526
44586CB00011B/433